POEMS FOR UKRAINE

POEMS FOR UKRAINE

AN ANTHOLOGY BY
POETRY PERFORMANCE
EDITED BY ANNIE HAVELL

Poetry Performance
An affiliate of Arts Richmond

First published in the UK in 2022 by Poetry Performance,
an affiliate of Arts Richmond
Edited by Annie Havell
Text & Design The Cutting Edge: www.tcecreative.co.uk
Publishers: Poetry Performance
Email: poetryperformancetw11@gmail.com

Individual poems copyright ©the authors 2022

Foreword ©Annie Havell

The moral rights of the poets to be identified as the authors of this work have been asserted by them in accordance with the Copyright, Designs and Patents Act 1988. All rights reserved.

No part of this publication may be reproduced or transmitted in any form or by any means, electronic or mechanical, including photocopying, recording, or any information retrieval system, without prior permission, in writing, from the publisher. This book is sold subject to the conditions that it shall not, by way of trade or otherwise, be lent, resold, hired out or otherwise circulated without the publisher's prior consent in any form of binding or cover other than that in which it is published and without a similar condition including this condition being imposed on the subsequent purchaser.

A CIP catalogue record is available from the British Library.
ISBN: 978-1-80068-983-1
Printed and bound by IngramSpark

To the people of Ukraine

CONTENTS

LIONEL BARTLEBY

    The Duckpond   14
    Why?   15
    Russian Warfare   16

TRISHA BROOMFIELD

    Bombs Fall   17
    The Wind Chills   18
    One Pound for Ukraine   18

PATRICIA CAMMISH

    Soniashnyk   19
    Putin—or Adverse Childhood Experience   20
    A Stripling Hope   22

PRATIBHA CASTLE

    In the Slips   24

ROBIN CLARKE

    It Only Needs One   25
    War Crimes   25
    Vladimir Putin   26

ANDREW EVZONA

    Ukraine's Burning   28
    Do You Leave, or Do You Stay?   29
    Don't Press It!   30

GREG **FREEMAN**

    Death Among the Conifers   31
    The Cricket Score   32
    The News from Ukraine   33

STEPHEN **GOSPAGE**

    Staged Event (Bucha, 1 April 2022)   34
    Missile   34
    Carnival   35

SHARRON **GREEN**

    Fear Flutters   36
    Thinking
    After Danusha Laméris   37
    I Feel...   37

STEPHEN **HARMAN**

    Promised Lands   38
    Anything Goes   40
    Brutal   42

Annie **HAVELL**

    Silence   43
    Медведь,   44
    President Putin   46

MATH **JONES**

    Peace   47

TONY **JOSOLYNE**

    Armorial   48
    Lost Sounds   48
    The Ukraine War   49

BOB **KIMMERLING**

    Ukraine's Tears   50
    Zoya's Tears   51

REINER **KUNZE**

    Ukrainian Night [Ukrainische Nacht]   52
    Song of the Thieves [Diebeslied]   54

BARBARA **LEE**

    We Watch   56
    Black Dust   57
    Free   58

KENNETH **MASON**

    A Mother's Plea   59

HEATHER **MOULSON**

    The Trouble With War   60

CHRIS **NAYLOR**

    Chlorine and Aleppo   61

DILLY **ORME**

    Unqualified   63

ALBERT **OSTERMAIER**

    Towards Kyiv and After [Nach Kiew]   64

JOHN **SEPHTON**

    War Child   66
    Unknown Soldier   66
    Hard Rain   66
    Apocalypse Now   66

FRAN **THURLING**

    Audience   67
    Kramatorsk Station, Friday 8th April 2022   68
    The War Goes On   69

ANN **VAUGHAN-WILLIAMS**

    Thoughts on Ukraine   70

CAROL **WAIN**

    Ukraine—Finding A Way Out?   72
    Ukraine—A Mother's Tale   73
    Ukraine—A Plea for Peace   75

KEITH **WAIT**

    Blue on Yellow   76

IAN **LEE-DOLPHIN** (SONG LYRICS)

    Get out of Ukraine, President Putin   78
    Vlad, Bad and Dangerous to Know   80

THE POETS   82

NOTES ON THE POEMS   98

FOREWORD

While the world gathered in Beijing to celebrate human achievement in sporting prowess, across Eastern Europe more ominous forces were amassing that would result in death and destruction, turning neighbour against neighbour, good friends becoming bitter enemies and the powerful 'Russian Bear' preying on the immortal 'Ukrainian Nightingale.'

People across the world have been shocked by subsequent brutal events. Even ordinary Russian citizens who, though able to hear the truth, are helpless in preventing the atrocities perpetuated in their name. Some Russian individuals have shown great courage in speaking out and even undertaking positive actions to help Ukrainians who are fleeing for their lives.

One such individual is Maria Emelianova, a photo journalist and chess master from Russia. Before the war began she was to fly to Croatia to receive her Pfizer Covid vaccination. Once the war began, however, she brought her flight forward a few days, thinking it would be better to leave sooner than later in case she was prevented from leaving by the Russian authorities, which subsequently happened to several of Maria's friends and relatives. Appalled by what she was seeing and hearing, she started raising money on her internet channel (twitch.tv/photochess) for Ukrainian refugees—this totalled US$ 135,000 from a single broadcast.

Maria is now *persona non grata* with the Russian authorities and faces a gaol sentence of at least fifteen years if she should return. She cannot go back home where her mother lives and doesn't know when she will see her again.

People all over the Western world, like Maria, are coming together to help the suffering of the Ukrainian refugees. Although every individual act of kindness could be seen as just a drop in the ocean, each drop comes together to form a wave of hope and compassion for all those fleeing the ravages of the war. Poetry Performance, a group of poets who meet regularly at the Adelaide Pub in Teddington, wanted to make their contribution to all these efforts. *Poems for Ukraine* is dedicated to the bravery, courage and steadfastness of the Ukrainian people.

Annie Havell
for Poetry Performance

All profits from the sale of this Anthology will go to *British-Ukrainian Aid, a charity providing humanitarian and medical aid to Ukraine in addition to supporting Ukrainian refugee artists.

*British-Ukrainian Aid:
charity registered in England and Wales 1164772.
www.british-ukrainianaid.org

ACKNOWLEDGEMENTS

Poetry Performance would like to thank all those who have provided help and support in the publishing of this anthology, including:

All the poets who have so generously contributed poems, reflecting their immediate response to the on-going war between Russia and Ukraine, including our two German poets, Reiner Kunze and Albert Ostermaier; and S. Fischer Verlag GmbH of Frankfurt am Main, for permitting Poetry Performance to reprint the poems for Reiner Kunze.

Tony Josolyne for his advice and support in helping collate the poems and for writing the description on the back cover.

Graham Harmes and his unstinting encouragement in every aspect of this poetry project.

Margaret May, who spent hours of research for her translations of the poems written by our two German poets.

Keith Wait for his introduction to Maria Emelianova, the chess player, who has done so much in helping to raise funds for Ukrainian refugees.

John and Heather Moulson for organising financial matters.

Our proof readers: Graham Harmes, Tony Josolyne, Margaret May, John Moulson.

Paul Warrington for his insights into graphic design, including the stunning cover artwork.

Peace

SWEET PEACE, where dost thou dwell ? I humbly crave,
Let me once know.
I sought thee in a secret cave,
And ask'd, if Peace were there.
A hollow winde did seem to answer, No:
Go seek elsewhere.

By George Herbert (1593-1633)

LIONEL **BARTLEBY**

The Duck Pond

For generations
We've all taken the little ones
Wrapped up in their
Pink woolly hats
And pink padded jackets
Or blue woolly hats
And blue padded jackets
Against the cold
To the pond in the park
To feed the ducks
It used to be bread
Now it's more environmental
We smiled at the little ones' strenuous throws
Often as not landing behind them
Or at their feet.
In Spring we smiled again
At the fluffy yellow chicks
Paddling line astern
After their Mum
Perhaps bumping into
Each other

The pond in the park
In Mariupol
Is now filled
With the debris
Of war
The ducks long gone
The people too

Dead

LIONEL **BARTLEBY**

Why?

'Why?'
My three-year-old self
Asked my Grandpa
'Why was there a World War Two
When you fought in the
War To End All Wars?'
'Ah!!!' he replied
After some thought

'Why is there Free Will?'
My five-year-old self
Asked the Vicar
'Ah!!!' he replied
After some thought

Why?
Asked my aged, irreligious self
Why is there no God
To curb one man's Free Will
Causing so many deaths?
After all he didn't know them
And all they wanted was
To live in peace
In Ukraine.

LIONEL **BARTLEBY**

Russian Warfare

An unexploded shell
Lay on the ground
Outside its target
An apartment block

A jostle of children
Desperate to escape the shelling
Ran out unheeding
The vibration of their running
Past the shell
Triggered its stuck fuse

Dust and silence settled
Ragged remnants of
Pink and blue padded jackets
Half faces, rent limbs and other human debris
Lay scattered all about

What right
Has any person
To perpetrate
Such atrocities

TRISHA **BROOMFIELD**

Bombs Fall (but not on us)

We sit on the floor
there is a war
bombs fall
but not on us
safe in our country at peace,
we watch the unwatchable
news unimaginable
tell each other not to look
yet look

we sit on the floor
in Ukraine there is a war
we, now hypersensitive
notice each other
as if for the first time.
I see your grey hairs
you see my older face
details in sharp focus denied
by day-to-day trivia

we sit on the floor,
over there is a war
we, cold inside, sit
in this pause of fear
while what matters
what really matters
holds our hearts
and bombs fall
but not on us.

TRISHA **BROOMFIELD**

The Wind Chills

The wind chills leaves before they're born
bites blossom buds before they're fully formed
birds fall silent, still and mourn
a peace filled day is slowly torn.

One Pound for Ukraine

...So I click 'Add one pound for Ukraine'
the self-service till smugly shuts down
'Oh it always does that,' says a helpful passer-by who
had the sense to queue.
I wait, foot tapping, time checking, hunger-panging
overburdened
for someone to come to my rescue
then, sunflowers by the door, surely not real
and I remember
foot weary, time lost, hunger pangs
overburdened, dying
for someone to come to their rescue
and I sigh,
'Add one pound for Ukraine'—
Is that really all I can spare!

PATRICIA **CAMMISH**

Soniashnyk

Bowed heads turn together, heavy,
insect thronged.
Corollas of gold face the sun,
tall and proud,
gleaming signs of peace.
Symbols of the riddance of the unthinkable
a generation back,
a riddance of toxic Soviet inheritance.
Then, as now,
signs of hope.
Their spiralled grains of life—
fecund, rich and ripe,
when crushed, bring forth
a precious flowing stream,
of golden gold.

The sunflowers stand defiant
against a sky of blue.
But broken, cut down,
will scatter a multitude of seeds into the wasteland,
a myriad germs of life,

PATRICIA **CAMMISH**

Putin—or Adverse Childhood Experience

The Kremlin hides a monster now
Who is not very tall.
Why is it true that men in power
Are often very small?

As if they need to bolster up
A lack of manly stature,
By proving to the world outside
They are the ones who matter.

An envious, spoilt, and puny youth,
Now skulks, where none can find,
Behind thick walls of steel and glass,
Compassion left behind.

The child is father of the man,
This warped and needy soul,
Invents, conceals, the truth to fit,
Omnipotence his goal.

Our early years define the rest—
The truest fact of life,
A barren, poisoned soil brings forth
A crop of joyless strife.

He's spent his life in showing off
And proving he's a hero,
With torso bared—he's diving in
Wild water at sub-zero.

Resentful, bitter, power mad,
Deluded, scarred within,
Reptilian deviate, arranging facts.
The world must bow to him.

'And I will do such things!' his cry,
'As on the earth ne'er seen.'
We know too well what danger lies—
We've read the lines between.

Pure might and strength he thinks is good,
His acts the world appal.
We creep and cringe—and dither now,
For fear he'll kill us all.

Is this the way the world will end—
By one demented hand?
A maniac taking all with him—
None left to understand?

PATRICIA **CAMMISH**

A Stripling Hope

Not long ago,
a fresh shoot emerged in this ravaged world,
a sapling, green, a stripling hope for the future,
not long ago,
last Halloween in Glasgow.
At Samhain, when souls may shift between worlds,
political posturing was almost set aside,
and the tide shifted—a little—
uncovering a hope
that nations might work together,
heed the warnings,
consider the future—others,
and the wider question—
the elephant on the planet.

A tender shoot, weak, uncertain,
but there,
a stripling growth,
set in soil not entirely welcoming,
but a hope, none the less,
burgeoning agreement
to gag
the toxic breath of commerce, industry, finance;
to quash the use of polluting products;
sacrifice something—
to preserve what we have.

Not three months later,
a flooding wave of war from the east,
indiscriminate,
brings devastation, destruction, death,
sanctions, shortages and threats unspoken.

The tide turns, shifts back.
The stripling hope withers.
Nations pull apart,
partisan in shameless scramble
for those same polluting products—
in the face of rising prices.

PRATIBHA **CASTLE**

In the Slips

While the world watches
Violetta, clad in years
the measure of a week,
journeys from Odessa
with her doll and cat

and a Grandma
her face a crumpled map
of lifetime drills
framed by a scarf
the colour of losing
urges a boy soldier
put this flower in your pocket

hopes his flesh
rotted into trampled mud
bone and blood
transmuted to
a claggy womb
will birth a crop
of smiling sunflowers

and men in black
as if spectators
at a cricket match
watch a tank
grizzle over cobblestones
across the city square
while a man
sprints into its path
scoops up a hand grenade
underarms it
at a pile of rubble
the dog-end
dangling from his lip
a red-eyed fuse

ROBIN **CLARKE**

It Only Needs One

One ruthless megalomaniac.
One superstate attack force.
One country—the target of invasion.
One head of state—to gallantly defend.
One small army—willing to resist or die.
One United Nations—to pontificate.
One group of western nations—to oppose and support.

Take away one megalomaniac?

War Crimes

Destruction, torture, rape, refugees.
Women killed, children killed, babies killed,
All Dead.
Maimed and mutilated.
Lives wrecked.
Soldiers ... misled, uninformed, confused,
 human, sub-human, animals, evil personified?
Genocide.

ROBIN **CLARKE**

Vladimir Putin

Who is this man called Vladimir Putin?
Who gave him the right to put the boot in?
His lies and falsehoods are all pervading,
Hidden truths beneath deceits parading.

Would his armies invade or not?
Some think he may have lost the plot.
He told the world he'd not invade.
So when he did, all felt betrayed.

Diplomacy was rejected,
By a tyrant defective.
Tanks then rolled in and missiles fired.
But Ukraine's resistance was inspired.

But what's his purpose in this war?
To change maps as they were before
In those days of the USSR?
He seems to act like some autocratic Czar.

But how can the West fight this peril,
A head of state who's now gone feral?
Sanctions seem to be the answer,
To combat this high-stake chancer.

He's now let loose the dogs of war.
Let's now let loose the dogs of law.
With crimes of war, we will charge him
For actions taken cruel and grim.

He's taken us to the brink,
Of world disaster, many think
Threatening with a nuclear weapon,
Armageddon now could threaten.

World's sympathy is with Ukraine
For their people's hurt and pain
Let war end soon, we hope and pray
And thus will dawn a peaceful day.

ANDREW **EVZONA**

Ukraine's Burning 2022

It's Winter and Ukraine's Burning
Vladimir Putin isn't for turning
He said it's a military operation
Could it be the end of a nation?

Years ago, it was part of the USSR
History dating back to the very first Tsar
A referendum was held in ninety-one
Its outcome did not please everyone

We recollect the disaster at Chernobyl
In eighty-six that so many would kill
Its radiation spread far and wide
With sadly, not a place to hide

Now, four decades on, another nightmare
More deaths and casualties, do we care?
We pray a solution can soon be found
Before Ukraine is burnt to the ground

ANDREW **EVZONA**

Do You Leave Or Do You Stay?

You've been invaded by a super power
You're about to enter your darkest hour
Your lives are in danger, you begin to pray
You must choose, do you leave or stay?

War has no care, and no rules are made
You need to survive, but are constantly afraid
Who knows what weapons will be used
And if civilians caught, will be abused.

Haunting air raid sirens are often heard
Can any country's leader keep their word?
Diplomatic solutions are better than destruction
Though just who will give the final instruction?

If you decide to leave, where do you go?
A neighbouring country may lessen the blow.
Your life is changed and will never be the same
There's reason for conflict and both sides to blame

Families dread the worst outcome of all.
There are no winners, backs 'gainst the wall.
Will someone resolve this—a new idea?
And bring to an end this suffering and fear.

ANDREW **EVZONA**

Don't Press It!

Please don't press the button
And blow our world to pieces
Let's try to find a solution
And pray hostility ceases

Nuclear Missiles should be banned
They threaten danger to us all
Leaders do need to understand
There are no winners, most will fall

We all live our lives in fear
Of a leader who's insane
Let's now make just one thing clear
Survival is the prize to gain.

GREG **FREEMAN**

Death Among the Conifers

This was once innocent,
Joan Hunter Dunn country.
Now behind the rhododendrons,
azaleas, conifers lurk foreigners
with something to hide, money,
identities. They try to conceal
themselves in woodland,
behind fairways. Occasionally
there's a mystery.

There may have been a court case,
or strangers in the neighbourhood.
A rich but shy man
is found dead in circumstances
not easy to explain away.
Another just the other day.
Terminated with impunity.
Foul play not suspected,
baffled police say, invariably.

GREG **FREEMAN**

The Cricket Score

In Hitchcock's The Lady Vanishes
Europe is on the eve of war
yet two Englishmen on the train
just want to know the Test match score.

Maybe that's why, after terrible scenes
of grief and suffering, and a Chinese
expert warning of nuclear holocaust
on Channel 4 News, plus the calming voice

of the weather forecaster, I switch to BT Sport,
England v West Indies in Antigua,
Barmy Army soaking up the Caribbean vibe,
England for once in the ascendancy,

just like in times long before, even
if it's most likely to end in a draw.
Ominous clouds, rain stops play.
Gardeners' World. Switch channels once more.

GREG **FREEMAN**

The News from Ukraine

I'll show those old ladies
mixing up Molotov cocktails,
bomb a nuclear plant
to a factor of ten Chernobyls.

These steroids pump
you up, help you
to see things
as they really are.

Never mind that bumbling
old man in the White House.
Never mind that clown we have
in place in Londongrad.

Never mind that our soldiers
don't know why they're there.
Look at little me, Ma!
Blowing up the world!

STEPHEN **GOSPAGE**

Staged Event (Bucha, 1 April 2022)

It wasn't that complicated,
But it had to be authentic.
No point in actors playing dead.
Think about it! They'll sneeze or twitch
As the cameras start rolling
And give the whole damn game away.
Luckily we had true patriots,
Prepared to sacrifice their lives,
Ready to jump in plastic bags
And take a bullet in the head.
Volunteers queued around the block,
Cheered on by happy families.
Who else would perform such a stunt?
Enemies are such nice people.

Missile

I popped out to the shops to buy some bread;
When I returned my family were dead.
A missile had destroyed our neighbourhood;
From this time onwards, nothing will be good.
I cannot understand these men of war;
I cannot comprehend what this is for.
We had no quarrel with our former friends;
How can these means advance their twisted ends?
Were they at war, my children and my wife?
They wanted no more than to live their life.
I search among the debris for a sign
Of those whose being intertwined with mine.
As I retreat beneath the cindered sky,
The hammer in my mind repeats: Why? Why?

STEPHEN **GOSPAGE**

Carnival

In time of war, things fit to you tightly:
No bagginess, no waste, no surplus slack.
War exposes us as human beings
And makes us face ourselves for what we are.
The carnival starts; you put on your mask
And run to meet your girl. Later, waking,
You hear a distant cry from your old friend,
Pleading for your help through the gas and mud.
But you are too warm; she is beside you,
Keen as a whip. The cry melts to silence.
Next day comes the knock. Sad entertainers
Dance quietly around the carousel.
In the mirror, you see your guilty grin
Fall down backwards, to where no one hears you.

SHARRON **GREEN**

Fear Flutters

Fear flutters in dawn's crimson light
Eyes struggle to absorb the sight
All sense is absent from this scene
The innocents have taken flight

What once was manicured and green
These busy streets, so ordered, clean
A testament to peace and love
Now ruined for a despot's dream

As bullets rain down from above
The tanks' contemptuous push and shove
Might—that is not for kinfolk meant
Now throttles with an iron glove

This evil war is bedlam bent
No justice to its foul intent
Why risk humanity for spite?
When will the tyrant pause, relent?

SHARRON **GREEN**

Thinking
after Danusha Laméris

Cheese on granary with coffee and grapes.
That'll be lunch. Digesting the latest.
But for now, I'm on a sunny dog walk.
Yellow gorse flags cerulean sky.

Should I have driven? Even electric?
Those eco-points expired quickly.
Better stock up on candles, toilet rolls,
flour, resilience... hospitality.

Dougie's throwing his weight around.
Pick on someone your own size!
They're escaping with dogs in handbags.
He'd have to walk—good puller and pillow though.

They hardly mention Covid now.
I'll sow sunflowers this spring.

I feel

awe at their bravery
sorry for their plight
angry that it's come to this
braced for a fight
horrified at Putin
anxious, sad and bleak
pity for the innocent
powerless and weak

STEPHEN **HARMAN**

Promised Lands

A call to arms
On strips of land and fields
Ancestors, friend or foe
Had farmed
Turned and sown
Tilled then
Churned again
Reaping more than
Any fork tongued politician
Could ever deem
To lend
Their soiled hands

The pain of war
On strips of land
And fields
Are raw
The cluster bomb and rifle butt
A bayonet's slash and cut
Gives nothing back at all
Save blood and tears
A solace less
Than any dove of peace
Would fly to guide
And rehabilitate or heal

These theatres of war
On strips of land
And fields
Abhor
Yet cannot be ignored
When diplomats
Count body bags
A Thousand high
In tragic piles

Near maps re-drawn
To illustrate
Not always liberate
Those countries now defiled
And when defined
Are left for others then
To orchestrate
In vain
Some catastrophic global change
Again.

STEPHEN **HARMAN**

Anything Goes

'In olden days
A glimpse of stocking
Was looked on as something shocking
Now heaven knows...'

Anything goes
Was the lead score
That became adored
By millions
In the musical
Of the same name
And written as a satire
To register the climate of the age

An urbane charming refrain
Cole Porter wrote the lyrics
In 1934
To counter the depression years
That had brought heartbreak and tears
As lives and fortunes simply disappeared
The song included the line
'The world's gone mad today'
And was written five years
Before a time that It really did
With slaughter brought on
By the second Great War

Now, once again
The generals' tanks
And the frenzied ranks of the media
Rap to the tune of the politicians' claptrap
And we are at it again
In Ukraine
West and East
Continue to compete

Their rights and wrongs
Set down in the songs
Of history
The lyrics
Written and re-written
Played out with the same old tunes
Laced in trust
Or mistrust
Dependent on your choice
Of hero or villain

And then
When the birds stop singing
'And anything goes'
The world holds its breath
And just hopes that
Not everything goes

STEPHEN **HARMAN**

Brutal

A new butcher's apron
Will look much the same
Viewed on a map
That is Earth's window frame
Resting there limp
With detritus and brain
For victor and vanquished
Their fate much the same

It hangs muted and deaf
Oblivious to pain
A cloth holding nothing
But hatred and shame
That slips neatly over
Those living and dead
Seeking only for power
Persecution and dread

And butcher will never
Discard his loose ends
But chops with a smile
To destroy once again
And woman and children
And ordinary men
Drip tears in his gravy
Until peace reigns again.

ANNIE **HAVELL**

Silence

I awake before sunrise and feeling an urge to walk,
    step outside into darkness.
All's eerily quiet, too early to hear the sounds of birds.
Where to go? Into the forest, where
perhaps there may be a stirring of life...
    the song of the Nightingale
or towards the town where one might hear
    the vroom of a motor car?
But no, silence reigns: the air remains still.
I don't like this silence,
    this feeling of being alone... disturbing.

I want company, I want to see people,
See them walking, smiling, gossiping.
The world has changed, I want that old world back,
Not this silent foreboding, this sense of loss.

This street, this town, this city has had its heart broken.
Go home! Go home!
Hear voices, reassuring voices telling us that
This country isn't broken: its spirit remains—
    angry, distressed, sad but
        Still it survives,
            unbroken.

ANNIE **HAVELL**

Медведь

The great bear, Медведь, has turned savage,
    letting loose the brutal dogs of war.
Unleashed they run amok, lusting for,
    smelling out human flesh, snarling when
    gazing into the gentle eyes of peace.

What you watch on your televisions,
    listen to on the radio, follow on social media
Isn't performance, staged especially for your
entertainment.
The blood you see that stains the streets
    was shed by living children, citizens, soldiers.
Buildings blasted by rockets, now lie in ruins —
    entombing dead bodies.
People seek safety in underground bunkers,
railway stations,
    car parks, cellars, under the stairs.
They flee to neighbouring countries.

Such is the theatre of War

We watch this slaughter play out on the telly,
    aghast at what we see on our screens.
We feel horror, sympathy.
 We rail at the oppressors, feel
    relief we're distant from that brutal theatre.
We want a David as told in that old bible story.

What price of freedom to rein in those dogs of war,
to tranquillise Медведь?

Медведь, take back your dogs!
Put them back on a leash.
Keep them under control.
Teach them to look into the eyes of peace
without flinching
    or send them back to hell, where they belong,
        back to the other hell hounds.

ANNIE **HAVELL**

President Putin
A Villanelle

President Putin—
    When invading the country of Ukraine
    Had you already envisaged end game...
    seizing lands, making them Russian terrain?

    Was this your first move—a foolhardy aim—
    An opening gambit? Forever you shame
    when invading the country of Ukraine.

    Western politicians say you're insane!

    Then blame NATO! Our resolve's the same:
    seizing lands, making them Russian terrain.

    We aren't Godless, and we are quite sane.
    Bishops pray daily to vanquish, not blame,
    when invading the country of Ukraine.

President Putin—
    Free speech is crushed in your brutal domain.
    Weak Russian pawns daren't call it a shame,
    seizing lands, making them Russian terrain.

    Envoi
    Sweet Nightingale you do not sing in vain.
    Your piping notes to Rooks tweet: 'Not Endgame'
    when invading the country of Ukraine,
    seizing lands, making them Russian terrain.

MATH **JONES**

Peace

This will be a difficult to write.
Needed to allow a touch.
Has to let a settle down.
Alightment. There.
Cannot put my legs. Walk
such a pasture. Hear
to the music. Help. Hand
needs taking and another
to the shoulder that I turn to,
burn to, fling so many hurts
away—only exhaustion of grief.
Only when I listen to the growing again,
and always it's a difficult to write.

TONY **JOSOLYNE**

Armorial

Arm,
Underarm, overarm
armour, arms,
armoury,
army, armada,
armistice, disarm;
re-arm, armaments...
Armageddon

Lost Sounds

Time and distance shield us
from cries of inhumanity and pain;
far from sight, unheeded,
they fade across the miles;
beleaguered, outskirts of the world,
discussed—but not suppressed.

The media present
scant glimpses of the truth,
stark images hit the screen
but the screams are muted out.

TONY **JOSOLYNE**

The Ukraine War

War-crimes
    Flattened: schools with children sheltering there.
    Destroyed: hospitals with expectant mums
    Slaughtered: captives with hands raised in the air.
    Assaulted: victims refuged in their homes.

Action
    Do leaders care about their soldiers' crimes
    and if they do, what action do they take?
    Is thought not paid to victims in these times,
    or mercy, when compassion is at stake?

    How can these evil acts serve any cause?
    Who pays the price for innocents who die
    and who is there to implement the laws?
    the families' survivors ask us why?

    Trained mainly in the ways to fight and kill—
    'humanity' seems off the syllabus;
    are blind eyes are turned to the invaders' will
    to loot and rape? The spoils of war—no fuss!

Retribution
    Beware! It's said, of Greeks when bearing gifts,
    'If offered sustenance, don't take your fill,
    Don't relax, in case the aggression shifts
    and those suppressed find their own ways to kill.'

BOB **KIMMERLING**

Ukraine's Tears

Those sun-kissed fields once filled with gold
now soak with soldier's blood,
and all her hopes and dreams of old
have been misunderstood.

Her women and her children flee
as freedom's breath grows faint,
and all the world in tears can see
as evil sheds constraint.

Dark shadows fall on Ukraine's fields,
her streets with rubble strewn.
Her children hide where dark conceals,
her scattered birds have flown.

Now West towards the setting sun
both child and mother flee.
So shield and shelter as they come
the outcast refugee.

And grant your shade from scorching heat,
give shelter one by one,
until oppression tastes defeat
with love's long battle won.

When he who tramples underfoot
has vanished from their land,
then He to whom this world must look
will take them in His hand.
Yes! He who wrote love's promise book
will bring His promised land.

BOB **KIMMERLING**

Zoya's Tears

Zoya sits, now all alone,
just staring through a window pane
to where a pink magnolia blooms
in someone else's garden.
And all her dacha's winter buds
are crushed and tombed in oil and mud
where tank and track has churned
and neighbours on their backs are burned
and seep her street and soil in blood.

Net curtains dim the window pane
but she can count each passing train
seen through the boundary hedge,
and glimpse each combed
and coiffured head
at eight, and half-past nine, and ten,
as Zoya sits upon a bed
and sees them coming home again
at five from Waterloo.

Her curtains flap in icy blasts
damp cushions lie in shards of glass
and where her gentle cat once basked,
A dog pack runs her street.
For Bucha and for Hostomel,
Her Kyiv's north Oblast,
Hot tears streak Zoya's cheek.

Although the hosts are warm, and kind,
Sweet Zoya is now seventy-nine.
Her smile conceals her inner tears,
her loss of ending peaceful years
sat gazing through her bedroom window,
towards her glowing sunflower fields,
her husband still asleep beside her.

REINER **KUNZE**

Ukrainische Nacht

Der Karpatenrücken ...
lädt dich ein
dich zu tragen
Rose Ausländer

Das land,
        verstümmelt,
                veruntreut,
                        verraten,
hob mich auf den rücken der Karpaten,
und im wachtraum hörte ich
        die dichterin die mutter fragen,
was diese gern geworden wäre, und die mutter sagen:
eine nachtigall

Da begannen alle nachtigallen
in den hainen, die ich in mir trug, zu schlagen,

und ich hörte schüsse fallen
und den namen widerhallen:
Maidan, Maidan

Und in des namens klang
klang der name an
des dichters, dessen wort wir in uns tragen:
Der Tod ist ein Meister aus Deutschland

Doch weiß man hier, der tod kam nicht
aus Deutschland nur, er kam
mit zweierlei gesicht,
und riesig ist das land, wo man
ihm blumen steckt und ruhmeskränze flicht

REINER **KUNZE**

Ukrainian Night

The Carpathians' back ...
invites you
to be carried
Rose Ausländer

The land,
    maimed,
        abused,
            betrayed,
lifted me onto the back of the Carpathians,
and in my daydream I heard her,
    the poet, ask her mother
what she'd have wished to be, heard her mother say:
a nightingale

Then all the nightingales in the groves,
that I bore within me, began to beat their song,
and I heard shots falling
and the name re-calling:
Maidan, Maidan

And in the sound of that name
his name too resounded,
the poet whose words we carry deep within us:
Death is a master from Germany

Yet here they know it came not, death,
from Germany alone, it also came
wearing a different face,
and immense is the land where they place
flowers for it and weave the victor's wreath

REINER **KUNZE**

Diebeslied

*Seit der Okkupation der Krim ...
findet nicht nur eine Verkehrung
der Tatsachen statt, sondern eine
Infragestellung der Tatsachen
selbst ... Die freche Lüge traut
sich auf die amtliche Pressekonferenz.*
Karl Schlögel

Zeig dem land, das dich betört,
das dir aber nicht gehört,
deine fürsorgliche liebe,
schenk ihm eine nacht der diebe,
die es stehlen ohne skrupel,
und verkünde dann mit jubel,
was dir pflicht war heimzuholen,
kann nicht gelten als gestohlen.

REINER **KUNZE**

Song of the Thieves

Since the occupation of Crimea...
not only are the facts turned
upside down, the very idea of fact
is called into question... brazen lies
are proffered at official press conferences.
Karl Schlögel

Show the land that so beguiles you,
but a land you do not own,
your caring love that soothes and calms,
give that land a night of thieves,
who steal it without any qualms,
and then all jubilant proclaim
what was your duty to reclaim
cannot be considered stolen.

BARBARA **LEE**

We Watch

We watch
We wait
Refugees at the gate

We watch
We wait
Will it be too late

We watch
We wait
We are at the other
side of the gate

We watch
We wait
Is it too late?

We watch
We wait
They knew their fate

We watch
We wait
Their pain
We ache

We watch
We wait
Help them
Through the gate.

We watch
We wait

BARBARA **LEE**

Black Dust

I don't see rockets
Or an attack
I don't see guns
Or sky that is black
With smoke and dust
And dirt and fumes

I don't see people
Cowering with fear
I don't see families torn apart with tears
I don't see homes burned to the ground
I don't see rubble all around

I see cars stopping
At red traffic lights
I see people walking
Home at night
I see tired faces
After a long day's work
I see innocence and kindness
No one is hurt

I see a future for my children
In the safety of our land
Playing on the sand
That is my plea
For them to be free

BARBARA **LEE**

Free

I got up this morning quite late
I had a shower
I had a cup of tea
I got ready to go to London
I am free

Did you see
The guns and soldiers on the streets
The homes of lovers, rubble and strewn
The children crying on the street
They are not free

Did you hear
The noise of sirens screaming loud
Voices of people in fear
They are not free

I'm going to London now
On a train
Pleased that I am free

KENNETH **MASON**

A Mother's Plea

I live at the top of this high rise block
wondering whether or not to stay.
All that I hear is tick-tock from my clock
as the drone from those aircraft fades away.

I really should walk down the stairs to the street.
The basement's much safer the soldiers say.
I'll just close my eyes to the blood by my feet.
A rocket or gun shell could kill us today.

Oh God keep my son safe, is my only prayer.
Though hardly a man, yet he's willing to die
to save our poor country from that evil slayer
that sits in the Kremlin saying war is a lie.

You in the rest of the world hear our plea.
We need you to help us remove this Red stain.
Send us some aid from way over the sea
and help us recover my beloved Ukraine.

HEATHER **MOULSON**

The Trouble with War

The trouble with war—
It distracts me from vital things
like my phone charger and blusher.
I don't know about this strange country
that sits vulnerably next to Russia.

The trouble with war—
are the Ukraine flag colours
that clash with my two piece
and my new designer shoes,
I'm not properly attired for peace

The trouble with war—
inconvenienced by casualties,
and devastation and outrage
in the broadsheets and The Sun.
Please kindly leave the page

The trouble with war—
families have to flee for safety
from bombs falling out the sky.
Filing my nails, I catch myself saying
there but for the grace of God go I!

CHRIS **NAYLOR**

Chlorine and Aleppo

When I look into your deep, green eyes
After more than a moment's passion,
As I lick the tears from your rosy, red cheeks
I know that you and your tears are pure
Because of—just a little Chlorine
In the water you had drunk, before we made love.

How dangerous suppose it would have been
If we had met in West Africa!
There you might have been black
And the moisture from your sweet, pink tongue
Could have been full of either E Coli, or Ebola or
perhaps both!

Suppose in the trenches, as lovers and mates
During a 'Gas Attack' I licked your Chlorine
contaminated tears
Streaming down your blue cheeks
Between outbursts of coughing and spluttering,
Then the green, the glorious and the clever Chlorine
Would have been the death of both of us.

And now in Syria, even this afternoon or tonight
The Bashar's regime prevents the delivery
Of Chlorine to water purification plants,
Instead it delivers deadly Chlorine to urban populations
From the air in bombs.

When Sir Humphry Davy discovered Chlorine
Would he have imagined its multiple duties?
First to protect us against microbes in
contaminated water
And preserve life,
Then as the basis for pharmaceuticals,
And a perpetual life in the new world of plastics
But again, as it did a hundred years ago
To kill us in warfare, as if we were wicked microbes,
In only thirty minutes!

As I find your body in our Aleppo street,
Your beautiful green eyes, now bloodshot
Our two children, dead in your arms
I'll poison myself and die beside you, as once again
I lick those tears from your now darkened, blue,
asphyxiated cheeks.

DILLY **ORME**

Unqualified

I do not feel qualified
To write about
The war in Ukraine.

It is insane.

The cruelty
The suffering
The pain.

I do not feel qualified
To write about
The war in Ukraine.

ALBERT **OSTERMAIER**

Nach Kiew
für jurij

du kriegst den krieg
nicht aus dem kopf
die kugel im herzen
durchschlägt die wände
der häuser der freunde
die es trifft mit dem
leben durch die haut
während du nur betroffen
bist und bleibst zuhause
in deiner betroffenheit
in deinem safe space
mit genügend raum für
deine panik die attacken
nach den bildern den
anrufen und rufen nach
mutiger hilfe die du und
wir verweigern unseren
frieden zu haben den sie
verteidigen an der front
unserer gewissenslosigkeit die
armeen unserer freiwilligen
sind worte wie diese waffen
ohne soldaten sie auf den
feind zu richten von dem
wir sagen er richtet sie
auch gegen unsere freiheit
die wir uns nehmen dass ihr
für sie sterben könnt mit ihr
was kann ich tun
wie schnell wird diese frage
vergangenheit sein
der konjunktiv II
unserer demokratie ich
lese tschechow bis mir
die tränen kommen wer
zu spät kommt der bestraft das
leben mit dem tod die panzer
rollen und die zeit läuft und
läuft und läuft und läuft läuft bis
sie abgelaufen ist
jetzt

ALBERT **OSTERMAIER**

Towards Kyiv and After
for yuriy

thoughts of the war
hammer in your head
the bullet in the heart
pierces the walls
of friends' houses
striking their lives
through their skin
while you are only
stricken and sit at home
in your stricken state
in your safe space
with enough room for
your panic attacks
after the images the
phone calls and calls for
valiant aid which you and
we refuse so as to have our
peace which they
defend at the front
of our lack of conscience the
armies of our volunteers
are words like these weapons
without soldiers targeting them at
the enemy of whom
we say he's targeting them
at our freedom too
which we take freely so that you
can die for it die with it
what can I do
how quickly this question will
pass into the past
the perfect conditional mood
of our democracy I'm
reading chekhov till my
tears come those who
come too late punish
life with death the tanks
roll and time runs and
runs and runs and runs runs until
it's run out
now

JOHN **SEPHTON**

War Child

Primal scream in the blood red snow,
whirlwind crossfire, the shattered citadel.
Tiny fragile heart beating hard,
mother weeping in the dark.

Unknown Soldier

unknown soldier
six feet under
absent without leave

Hard Rain

dark knights in armour
mad bears marching on to war
longbowmen at the border
a hard rain's gonna fall

Apocalypse Now or Heart of Darkness

Ride the Valkyries
to the heart of darkness,
the lost wilderness,
the twilight kingdom,
the shadow of death.
Terminate with prejudice
the hollow man,
the horror.

FRAN **THURLING**

Audience

Pounded by image we sit and watch a country bleed,
our days peaceful,
our nights without sirens.

May we ask you when do you decide to leave?
After how many sleepless nights,
flattened cities,
broken lives,
shattered dreams?

And how will you go?
Squashed onto trains, buses, into cars?
On foot over makeshift bridges,
past barricades and checkpoints,
dodging fire?

And what will you take?
Your children, memories, fear, despair, the will to live,
hope for some future?
Fingers crossed.
We keep watching.

Who wrote this pitiless script?
Refugees fleeing a wasted homeland.
Real, unreal, too real.

FRAN THURLING

Kramatorsk station, Friday 8th April 2022

But why are they here at the station, these people?
The mothers and children, all here at the station?
And old folk?
All at the station, all milling.
It can't be for working, maybe for a trip?
Excursion, one not to be missed.
So why are they fearful and why are they crying?
And wanting to get on that train, oh so much?
So much has happened.
Lives are in pieces.
Oh...

'Go now,' said the leader, get out while you can.
They come, they keep coming, in hundreds
and hundreds.
To get on a train that may be the last one.
To get on a train, to escape while they can.
They are close.
Getting closer.
Don't panic!
Don't push!

Shell

Strikes

FRAN **THURLING**

The War Goes On

The war goes on. Destruction. Death.
There are bodies. It is war. People die.

Who are they? How did they die? Is it a war crime?
Is it a crime? Is this war a crime?
Is war a crime?

It is war. It goes on. Its consequences ripple
and rumble around. Round the world. There
are ramifications. Disruptions, interventions,
statements, discussions, predictions, shortages,
sanctions, prognoses, explanations, condemnations,
justifications, analyses, protests… It goes on.

Blow by blow reports go on. 24/7. People die. It goes
on. It is war. With a ringside world. A grandstand view.
24/7 commentary. Reporters are on to it. On the
ground. In the studio. Updates. It goes on. 24/7.
Misses and hits. Destruction. Death. Hits. Misses.
Interviews. Survivors, politicians, bystanders, victims,
hospital staff, volunteers, international agencies,
witnesses, refugees, next of kin… People die.
It goes on.

It doesn't stop. It goes on. People die. It is war.
Wasteful. Wanton. It's not a game. Not a film.
Not a page in a history book. Destruction. Death.
There are bodies. It goes on.

And grief.
It goes on.

ANN **VAUGHAN-WILLIAMS**

Thoughts on Ukraine

The buildings are twisted frames
Everything burnt in explosions,
Whole cities bombed to shreds.

People collect in a theatre
For safety—only to be bombarded—
Leaving only bodies and rubble.

In the zoo
A child rides a camel—
Normal pleasure briefly restored.

Queues form to join the exodus—
People leaving their land
Wrapped in warm clothing for the snow,

A woman cradling her cat,
A child clutching a hand,
Each person carrying one bag from the wreckage.

We who live freely cannot imagine
The shock, the panic when there is
the necessity of leaving.

One woman was head blasted,
Cannot remember anything, shocked
Feels no emotion.

We watch it on our television,
Remember bomb sites in London,
Remember rebuilt housing estates in Coventry

Remember the small post war ration of cheese,
One precious bar of chocolate.
See the apple trees re-growing where a bomb dropped

Remember meeting grandparents
Not seen in five years,
Joy of belonging.

Our civilization
Could be reduced to rubble
Full of poisoned bodies.

Will our ruins be visited
By future survivors
Who will gasp at the stones of old cities?

And will there be children who learn about Putin
The man who reduced the Western world
To a shadow of itself?

CAROL **WAIN**

Ukraine—Finding a Way Out?

These past five weeks it's hogged our screen

On prime-time news. Sitting here in comfort,
We can't escape the images: destruction,
Blackened buildings, the dead—unless
We turn off our TVs...

Always there on mobile phones or tablets,
Plastered over newspaper front pages,
Stirring up vague memories of the Blitz
From grainy newsreels, or nineties Bosnia.
"Have you forgotten Syria?"—they ask.

Then someone high up talks of nuclear threat,
Recalling the Cuban Crisis when I was 20.
Sons and daughters, millennials, faced with fear anew,
Are hit with angst, they drink, can't sleep.
I worry how it will affect my son.

Return to news—but only once a day,
Curtailing it to try to keep us sane—
Therapy from squirrelling reserves for refugees—
We take them to the Centre where they sort it
To send on. Released, we gladly walk away.

The News again: perhaps they've found a way
To settle the impossible—can Putin save his face?
By giving him those territ'ries claimed to be
His own, where most speak Russian after all:
It seems that a solution may be made...

More refugees are leaving, so then a line is drawn.
We settle down to sleep, burying our heads once more...

[72]

CAROL **WAIN**

Ukraine—A Mother's Tale

That crisp next morning, early, we wake to engine
   noises
Helicopters low flying overhead—I firmly warn my
   children:
"Do not go outside." They stay indoors and play with
toys,
    make models, while I follow the news, anxiously—
"It's a national emergency: we are at war. Be brave
   but safe."

My husband signs for our militia: he trains,
   and patrols near city limits. I'm not sure
When I'll see him again—if EVER. The kids don't ask.
Shooting starts, rockets fire above—just one week
   on—
We hear loud bangs, see smoke, and then we move…

To the underground, for shelter. Hear that a lady in
   our flats
   brought down a Russian 'copter, waving her
   broom at it!
We take along our Husky dog, Pyotr, with Persian cat.
We pull cases, tins of petfood, coffee,
Children's books, one best toy each, our warmest
   clothes, water…

Days pass, don't know if home still stands—
Food arrives, news in snippets: our boys so brave.
Ukraine still holds—Kharkiv and Mariupol under fire—
Where is my man? Shut the thought, just survive…
Talk of a ceasefire, a lull—few hours to help us escape

To safety 'cross the border: shelled beneath a bridge,
   but make it, trembling, to a coach: cat and Pyotr
   with us,
One case each, scramble frantically though narrow
   door—
Drive away down shell-strewn roads—to where?
The Polish border, through darkened forests, family
   in Krakow.

Haunted yet secure in Poland, we cannot know our
   future.
The kids enrol in school, sleep well, but miss their
   father.
I blindly study 'situations vacant.' When will this end?

CAROL **WAIN**

Ukraine—A Plea for Peace

Amidst the shooting, bombs and destruction,
Hollowed out buildings and pitted streets,
Families, mothers, the old ones, cry out for peace.

Where are the efforts to bring both sides together?
Why has the world not done its utmost
To sue for peace—have they forgotten them for ever?

Stop the bombastic language, let calm words prevail;
Some of them escaped, leaving others stuck in fear,
Behind barbed wire in windowless, empty flats.

In those dark basements they yearn for a return
To normal days of shopping, love and laughter;
War leaders to reconcile and yield some new ground.

As somebody once sang, all we need is love—
And so we pray for an outbreak of peace...

KEITH **WAIT**

Blue on Yellow

We waded waist-deep in waving wheat-fields
Gently, so not to damage precious stems
To seek the singing in the sunflowers
To dance in this beloved land,
Its soil, a golden yellow band.
Beneath a deep blue sky
Yellow and blue fly high.

High on steeples, domes and humble cottage
How proudly waves the flag of precious home
To show our souls are full of happiness
In cities that we call our own.
Atop our towns the flag is flown
For families we love,
For those it flies above.

24th February 2022

Now blasted, bombed-out, burning, buried
The tyrant irredentist steals our spring
Wheat stems to shattered stubble, sunflowers
Stunted in a ravaged landscape
Its soil tortured by tank tracks.
Beneath a blackened sky
Wings of death fly high

Steeples splintered, domes destroyed bear witness
To precious homes all gone. We starve. We freeze.
Our people's tears are full of bitterness
For husbands killed and wives defiled
For children orphaned and the weak exiled.

One man can rant and lie
And send his sons to die.
But he has predation;
And we have devotion.
He has total carnage;
We have only courage.
He loves hot fire and blood
While we are fired by love.

So blue and yellow flies above
Riddled.
Fly blue for bravery
And yellow now for love.

IAN **LEE-DOLPHIN**

Get out of Ukraine, President Putin

A Song for Ukraine

President Putin
President Putin
You've got power and wealth
But you've lost the plot

You've lost the plot
You've lost the plot
You've invaded Ukraine
And what have you got

What have you got
What have you got
You've got rising inflation
And thousands of dead

CHORUS:
Come take your troops back home
Your armoured trucks and your cluster bombs, go home
Do the decent thing
And LEAVE

Queuing for Poland
Queuing for Poland
Women and children
Are all getting out

All getting out
All getting out
They don't want Putin
From the North to the South

The North to the South
And the East to West
President Putin
Oh what a mess

Repeat CHORUS

Get out of Ukraine
Get out of Ukraine
President Putin
Get
Out
Of
Ukraine

IAN **LEE-DOLPHIN**

Vlad, Bad and Dangerous to Know

A Song for Ukraine

Mr. Putin
What are you doing?
Are you bad, are you bad, are you bad?
Mr. Putin
What are you doing?
You've ruined it for everyone

You've bombed churches
You've bombed schools
Aren't you sad, aren't you sad, aren't you sad?
You've killed women
You've killed children
Are you mad, are you mad, are you mad?

You've let the World down
You've let the Ukraine down
Are you glad, are you glad, are you glad?
You've let your Country down
You've let your family down
But most of all, you've let down yourself

Mr. Putin
What are you doing?
Are you mad, are you mad, are you mad?
Mr. Putin
What are you doing?
You are mad, bad and dangerous to know

The Poets

A poet is a person who holds views on life today,
imagines life in the future
against the backdrop of life in the past.

THE POETS

LIONEL **BARTLEBY**
Lionel graduated with a degree in Chemistry. After a varied career spanning both the sciences and humanities he had to take early retirement. The *Guardian* had an article on finding one's 'voice' through poetry. For a number of years Lionel wrote and performed with a poetry group, and some of his work was published. His life then moved in other directions although he continued to write, particularly about growing old and the new perspectives it gives you on the great poetic themes. Lionel has performed some of this poetry at the Adelaide Pub to bring his work to a wider audience.

My Poems
From the early TV reports of the Ukraine conflict, three images in particular caught my attention: the women and children getting off the trains in Poland, just ordinary people; the pink and blue padded jackets of the little ones; and the smoke-blackened apartment block façades. For as long as I can remember, I have posed the question 'Why?' with regard to people's motivations. 'Russian Warfare' came from watching 'UXB' (unexploded bomb) on television and realising just how dangerous faulty unexploded ordnance can be.

TRISHA **BROOMFIELD**
Trisha has had three poetry pamphlets published by Dempsey and Windle and has contributed to Surrey Libraries Poetry Blog, Surrey Libraries Words in Focus and Places of Poetry. She read regularly on her local radio during 2020/2021 and has contributed to BBC Radio Surrey. In 2021 Trisha was short-listed for the Roger McGough Poetry Prize, performing with other finalists at The Exchange in Twickenham. Her poems can be found on Facebook, *Trisha Broomfield Poetry, Instagram magentapink22*. She has also been featured on the online magazine 'Spilling Cocoa over Martin Amis'. Observation and humour make up most of her work.

My Poems
Bombs Fall: This poem was written while sitting on the floor with my husband watching the awful news about the bombing in Ukraine. These were early days and the constant news had not had time to numb us, and we felt it deeply.

The Wind Chills: I wrote the poem one morning after watching the news. I could think of no other way of expressing myself. The images were dreadful, but we had all seen them. I felt that everything that could be said had been said and there really were no words to convey the horror unfolding before us.

One Pound for Ukraine: I devised this poem in my head after heading for the self-service till to pay for food. Once at the till these two words appeared on the screen encouraging a donation for Ukraine, 'One pound'. I tried to comply, the machine shut down, I was in a rush, lunchtime, and while I waited for a member of staff to come to my aid I noticed sunflowers in a bucket by the entrance. I thought about those people in Ukraine waiting for a rescue that may never come. I felt humbled, my contribution paltry.

PATRICIA **CAMMISH**
Patricia was born in the grey back streets of the post-war industrial north, but within easy reach of the Peak District, She developed an early love of the wild, rocky beauty of the natural world and its counterpart in literature. Pat has always enjoyed words and languages and, after a career in Education, she now has time for travel, grandchildren and, of course, writing, both poetry and prose. Many of Pat's poems have appeared in poetry anthologies including 'Identity' (Roger McGough poetry competition) and 'Through the Keyhole.'

My Poems
Russia's invasion of Ukraine, the most recent of Russia's forays into empire building, delves deep into the human psyche, strips bare the veneer of civilisation. Why we are so concerned this time? The answers, full of home truths, are shameful.

PRATIBHA **CASTLE**

Pratibha Castle's award-winning debut pamphlet A Triptych of Birds and A Few Loose Feathers (Hedgehog Poetry Press) was published February 2022. Her work appears in Agenda, HU, Blue Nib, IS&T, London Grip, OHC, Friday Poem, High Window, Lime Square Poets, Live Encounters Poetry & Writing, and Dreich, amongst others. Pratibha's work has been highly commended and long-listed in a number of competitions, including The Bridport Prize and Welsh Poetry Competition, Sentinel Literary Journal, Brian Dempsey Memorial Award, Binsted Arts and Storytown. A regular reader for The Poetry Place, West Wilts Radio, she is featured on Home Stage: Meet the Poet.

My Poem
In the Slips: In the early days of the invasion, the personal reports I read touched me greatly. All of the events in the poem, In The Slips, are inspired by real events.

ROBIN **CLARKE**

Robin says that any talent he has for writing poetry was inherited from his mother. He started writing poems when working for the bank, either to celebrate birthdays or to mark someone's departure. His poems have been published in a jazz magazine and church magazines. He has also contributed to two Anthologies, 'Where the River Rests' and 'Through The Keyhole.' His leisure interests include ballroom dancing, traditional jazz and conversational French.

My Poems
I was inspired to write poems relating to the Ukraine conflict and eventual war by the ever-increasing tension prior to the invasion shown in the press and then the invasion itself and the consequent devastation that followed. The duplicity of Putin and his government to mislead the Russian people, the Russian soldiers; and their attempt to fool the rest of the world was unbelievable. The harrowing images of destruction of cities and the tragic interviews with the survivors telling their stories add to the horror of this continuing conflict.

ANDREW **EVZONA**
Born of Greek Cypriot parents, Andrew enjoys travel and likes all types of sport and has run in four London Marathons. He started working as a Cover Supervisor Supply Teacher for Reed Management in November 2020 after being furloughed from the Business Travel Industry. He also works for Opogo and TradeWind in the same teaching capacity. Andrew has published two books, the second of which, '300 POEMS TO MAKE YOU T.L.C. (think, laugh and cry)' was published in December 2021 with some of the proceeds going towards Diabetes and Dementia charities.

My Poems
Having a wife with Russian origins and having visited Russia several times, the current situation, as described by the media, fills me with mixed feelings. I understand that Putin has deep concerns about Ukraine and its potential wish of becoming a member of NATO, an organisation that Putin fears as he considers it a threat to Russia. I can't believe, however, that warfare will resolve this. The resultant suffering and destruction will not be to anyone's advantage. The background threat of nuclear action is too horrific to envisage and cannot be the answer to any political disagreement.

GREG **FREEMAN**
Greg Freeman is a former newspaper sub-editor, and now news and reviews editor for the poetry website Write Out Loud. He has published one full collection, *Marples Must Go!* (Dempsey & Windle, 2021), and two pamphlets, *Trainspotters* (Indigo Dreams, 2015), and *The Fall of Singapore* (Dempsey & Windle, 2022). He also co-comperes a twice-monthly open-mic poetry night, Write Out Loud Woking, at the Lightbox art gallery in Woking, and on Zoom.

My Poems
In the first weeks of the war in Ukraine, I wrote a number of poems about it. I could write about nothing else. They were angry poems, based on what I had seen on news bulletins, and of the moment, somewhat dashed off, full of contempt and hatred for Vladimir Putin, the new Hitler in our midst. I would put 'The News From Ukraine' in that category. After a while I found I couldn't write that sort of poem any more, even though the atrocities discovered grew

even worse. 'The Cricket Score' came from a sense of guilt. 'Death Among the Conifers' takes us back to Putin and his henchmen. Surrey was once thought of as John Betjeman country, the home of Joan Hunter Dunn, synonymous with safety, if not complacency. Yet in recent years an unusually high number of Russian oligarchs who have sought refuge in or just moved to Britain, and Surrey in particular, have been found dead in their luxury homes in mysterious circumstances. You think of the Salisbury poisonings, and you wonder about those oligarch/fugitives who may have been somehow assisted to hang themselves; and you reflect on what a deeply unpleasant gangster Putin actually is. We have turned too many blind eyes in the past, including ignoring atrocities the Russians themselves committed in Syria. We can't do that anymore. I would only add that my latest poetry collection, The Fall of Singapore, was published almost exactly at the same moment as the invasion of Ukraine. There are a number of poems in that pamphlet with wartime settings that suddenly acquired a grim new relevance.

STEPHEN **GOSPAGE**

Stephen Gospage, a writer of poetry and short stories, was born in London in 1953 and spent most of his working life in Brussels. Now retired, he lives in Belgium, close to Waterloo. He has dual British and Belgian nationality and is proud to call himself a citizen of Europe. Several of his poems have appeared in the New European newspaper and he is a regular contributor to the Write Out Loud poetry blog.

My Poems

'Staged Event (Bucha, 1 April 2022)' was written after hearing a Russian Government spokesman describe the gruesome discovery of bodies of civilians in Bucha as a 'staged event'. I wanted to satirise the crass absurdity of this claim by imagining how, in a topsy-turvy world of amoral inverted logic, someone might have 'staged' such an event.

'Missile' is about grief expressing itself through incomprehension. During a war, people still have to go out to find food. Commerce still tries to function. A missile strikes, seemingly completely random, from the point of view of civilians. Tragically, we see this played out in real time on television. So here a man pops out for some bread and comes back to find his home and family destroyed.

'**Carnival:**' nobody (or almost nobody) wants war. Peace should be the normal state of affairs, not conflict. Yet wars happen and some people will choose, or be forced, to fight, while others, for whatever reason, will not face the dangers of battle. This situation is bound to lead to feelings of resentment or guilt. Although the contrast between the horror of war and the joys of the carnival is obvious enough, this poem tries not to take sides on the issue.

SHARRON **GREEN**
Sharron Green describes herself as a 'poet of a certain age' and shares poetry with elements of nostalgia, attempting to make sense of modern life and celebrate nature. She enjoys experimenting with rhymes and poetic forms.

Sharron has had poems published in over ten international anthologies. 'Viral Odes' is her chapbook of pandemic poems, currently available via her website and online from most bookshops. In 2021 she completed an MA in Creative Writing at the University of Surrey and is now gathering poems for a new collection.
Instagram, Facebook & Twitter: @rhymes_n_roses
Website: https://rhymesnroses.com

My Poems
Along with many poets feeling helpless and scared about the Ukraine War, Sharron has written about it as a way to record her feelings and channel the anxiety. As @rhymes_n_roses on Instagram she posted *Fear Flutters* and *I feel* in response to prompts. *Thinking after Danusha Laméris* was set as homework on a City Lit Advanced Poetry course and reflects the thoughts that surface whilst completing mundane tasks.

STEPHEN **HARMAN**
Although Steve's academic background is in the Social Sciences, he has always enjoyed the arts and literature. He strongly believes a poem enables the writer to condense life into snapshots of our own

thinking and being. It offers in just a few words an attempt to make sense of the emotions and imagery we all feel in our subjective and external worlds or situations... a chance to stir and reflect on those feelings drives the quest to achieve the poem's goal.

My Poems
In '**Anything Goes,**' I was interested in the build-up to conflict in general while life goes on regardless: a lull before the storm—in this case WWII.

'**Promised Lands**' attempts to demonstrate the futility of war: the geographic gains and losses that are played out alongside the tragedy where friend can become foe in the futile wretchedness of it all.

In '**Brutal**' we see the catastrophe of what happens when lunatics are allowed to take over the asylum at the highest political level. The vulnerability and destruction of the masses when following, or falling victim to despots at any given period in history.

ANNIE **HAVELL**
Annie has sauntered through a number of diverse employments since leaving school, including telephonist, actress, youth leader, teacher, lecturer, reviewer. Since retirement she has focused more strongly on her great loves, drama and poetry, working as a drama judge for Arts Richmond, and establishing Poetry Performance.

My Poems
The symbolism of Russia's great brown bear, Медведь, and the national bird of Ukraine, the common little Nightingale, reminded me of the battle between David and Goliath, as told in one of the old testament stories in the Bible. In my poem, 'Mr Putin,' I was influenced by Maria Emelianova, the chess player, remembering that both Russia and Ukraine are great chess playing countries: the Villanelle, with its strict rules, seemed an appropriate form for the poem. In Edwin Muir's famous poem, 'The Horses' the all-pervading atmosphere is that of silence, and I was reminded of this when hearing about the plight of all those Ukrainians forced to live under ground for weeks on end, hence my poem 'Silence.'

MATH **JONES**
Math has written poetry all his life, but only really noticed that recently, acting is now the career he's focused on. He's worked years as a bookseller, in London, Brighton, and Worcester, and it was amidst the Worcester poetry circle that he began to take his writing and the performing of it seriously. Two books published: 'Sabrina Bridge,' and 'The Knotsman.'

My Poem
'Peace' was written in response to a Wombwell Rainbow prompt and is as much about its acceptance as its existence. Healing from trauma needs the knowledge that the cause of trauma has gone; silence might only last till the next siren goes. And the shock of accepting that peace prevails can be as jolting as a lightning strike, with flashbacks perhaps being a recognition of coming into a safer place, of seeing more life happening.

TONY **JOSOLYNE**
Following four years as a Radar mechanic in the RAF became an Electronics Engineer with Decca Radar and Navigator Companies, moved on to become a Lecturer at Carshalton College. He also spent ten post-retirement years with Richmond College.

My Poems
The news about Russia and Ukraine was made very clear on TV and by the newspapers. As a child during WW2, in 1941 I had survived, under the stairs, with my family, when our house in Wallasey was blitzed. I also have a clear memory of those final nuclear attacks on Hiroshima and Nagasaki. Later, as an adult, I learnt of the terrible aftermath from radioactive exposure, suffered by the islanders.

The falsehoods and veiled threats of nuclear escalation from Vladimir Putin progressed very quickly to Russia's attack on Ukraine. My initial response of disbelief and worry led to a few lines of poetry that I discarded very quickly: too much to say and none of it inspiring. Before managing to produce something to summarise the terrible attacks by the Russian army, I found some earlier poems that share my overall feelings about warfare.

BOB **KIMMERLING**
Bob Kimmerling has lived in Richmond with his family since 1980. He has been a minister at the Vineyard Life Church until recent retirement but remains a director of the Vineyard Community Centre and the Richmond foodbank. Bob started writing poetry just before Covid lockdown and published his first memoir book, 'Fishing for Dr Richard' in Nov 2021.

My Poems
'Ukraine's Tears' was written first and inspired in March by some verses in Isaiah 16 vs 3-5.
> "Hide the fugitives,
>   do not betray the refugees.
> Let the Moabite fugitives stay with you;
>   be their shelter from the destroyer."

'Zoya's Tears' was written after getting to know Zoya and the circumstances of her evacuation from Kyiv to Prague, and then her arrival at Stansted on March 12th to join her daughter in Richmond.

Zoya had property in Ukraine, a comfortable life in Kyiv, and a country dacha in Hostomel. She used to lecture in engineering at Lviv University and had retired with her husband, a scientist of some renown, who died two years ago in April 2020. She expected to live out her years peacefully but has suddenly faced the loss of everything. Though coming to a place of safety, Zoya does not want to be here. Aged 79 she grows increasingly homesick no matter how welcome she is made. She speaks little English and though on the outside Zoya is remarkably resilient, putting on her best face in public and trying to join where invited, on the inside there are many tears.

Richmond and SW London has the highest number of Ukrainian refugees arriving in this country. The borough may welcome several hundred, nearly all women and children or teenagers. Most will have some trauma, most will be homesick, and most will have the concern of menfolk and family who remain.

REINER **KUNZE**
Reiner Kunze was born in 1933 in Oelnitz, Eastern Germany as the

son of a miner. He graduated from Leipzig University in philosophy and journalism. In 1977 he moved to the Federal Republic of Germany. He published various poetry volumes and the much translated prose volume *Die wunderbaren Jahre* with S. Fischer Verlag and was awarded many literary prizes, among them the Georg Trakl prize, the Geschwister Scholl Prize and the renowned Georg Büchner Prize.

The two poems reprinted here are from Reiner Kunze: die stunde mit dir selbst
© S. Fischer Verlag GmbH, Frankfurt am Main, 2018. All rights reserved by S. Fischer Verlag GmbH.
(978-3-10-397376-1)
Translations by Margaret May.

BARBARA **LEE**
Barbara works as a tutor for adults whose English is not their first language. In the past she has undertaken a variety of sporting volunteering roles including 'Games Maker' for the London Olympics in 2012, the Commonwealth Games in Glasgow, the Ryder Cup in Gleneagles and later this year, the Birmingham Commonwealth Games. She has also worked as a warden during the Summer months at Buckingham Palace. Currently Barbara is running creative and poetry workshops. She has just discovered her singing voice and sings in three choirs.

My Poems
I was prompted to write about Ukraine because I was seeing a country and people whose lives suddenly have taken a different path over which they have very little control. It was this that I wanted to bring out in my poems. Each day we make plans and think about where we are going, what we're doing—everyday things like work, shopping or getting excited about seeing family and friends. I felt so dreadful about all those emotions being shut down, perhaps forever, for so many Ukrainians, so I wrote simply about going to London. I thought deeply about what I would do and feel if all of a sudden I had no control over my life. Those images of children on a train, and the sense of loss and grief I felt for the Ukrainians suddenly overwhelmed me. I just wanted it all to be rewound, for those people to go once again shopping, to go to work and for their children go to school... to be free.

KENNETH **MASON**
For the past four score years Ken say he has ambled through various employments, from working on a farm to route intelligence for an airline to chimney sweeping to becoming an actor to modelling in advertising to owning a toy-shop to furniture restoration to writing plays. The joy has been meeting such diverse groups of people on the journey.

My Poem
One evening, while I was watching the news on TV, a Ukrainian woman was being interviewed describing the appalling conditions she was living in. Many of her words have been used in my poem as I felt she and the words she spoke should not be forgotten.

HEATHER **MOULSON**
Heather is one of the founder members of Poetry Performance in 2017. Since then she has written and performed extensively in London, Woking and Guildford. Heather often describes herself as living with a grumpy black cat, Dobby, whom she constantly draws. Many of these drawings are in her published book. 'Conversations with Dobby!' Heather's first pamphlet 'Bunty I Miss You' was published in 2019. She also writes Theatre and Poetry reviews for the 'Mark Aspen Reviews' on-line site.

My Poem
My poem is a response to all the war reports that come into our homes through the mass media and my observation of how some people are unmoved, feeling inconvenienced.

CHRIS **NAYLOR**
Chris Naylor is a retired consultant obstetrician and gynaecologist. Brought up on a farm in Mid Wales he came to London in 1964 to complete his postgraduate studies. He regards himself as a 'townie' and would not be able to pursue his interests in opera, the theatre and food back in the countryside. He has travelled widely in a professional capacity and for pleasure sailing in the Caribbean, Turkey, Greece, Thailand and the Seychelles. He is an

accomplished skier. With his wife Vicki, they run a weekly writers' meeting. A couple of years ago he wrote and produced his first play, 'See Me for Myself.' It had a four-week run at The Tabard Theatre in Chiswick. Currently he is editing his first novel, 'No Exit' based on his experiences in Saudi Arabia.

My Poem
My poems come ready formed, and the subjects are usually moral. Currently I am considering a poem about severe illness in Heads of State, using Putin's reputed cancer of the thyroid and metastases in his brain as an example. If the prognosis is poor, a Head of State's determination to bring about their ambitions for their own country regardless of how this will affect the rest of the world, is an issue that requires world-wide discussion.

DILLY **ORME**
Dilly Orme lives near Hampton Court with her two gorgeous 'on the brink of nest flying' daughters and is presently having an adventurous time dating. She earns her living as a stylist and writer, contributing regularly to all the mainstream interiors magazines including 'Ideal Home' and 'House Beautiful' and has a weekly craft column in 'My Weekly.' Personally she is very interested in people and their stories and has enjoyed encapsulating those and expressing her own in poetry since childhood, feeling It is a wonderful unifying way to distil ideas and tell succinct tales.

ALBERT **OSTERMAIER**
Albert Ostermaier was born in 1967 in Munich, where he now lives. He is a prolific writer and has produced 12 volumes of poetry (the latest, *Teer* [Tar] was published in 2021), 39 plays, seven libretti and four novels. He was playwright-in-residence at the Nationaltheater in Mannhein and at the Bayerisches Staatsschauspiel in Munich, writer-in-residence at New York University in 2001, and a visiting lecturer at various German universities. He gained a high reputation as the artistic director of different festivals, and has won prestigious awards for his work, including the Ernst Toller Prize 1997, the Kleist Prize 2003, and the Bertolt Brecht Prize 2010.
Translation by Margaret May.

JOHN SEPHTON
John Sephton started writing poems during breaks in walks in the countryside. Influenced by Japanese haiku and the clear precise writing of authors such as Hermann Hesse, his style has evolved over the years, and he focuses now on writing short poems that aim to convey powerful imagery and emotion in a concise manner.

My Poems
Appalled by the images of death and destruction caused by Putin's invasion of Ukraine, he was inspired to write several poems in the above style.

FRAN THURLING
Fran remembers enjoying reading and writing poetry as a young child. She rediscovered this interest in writing poetry a few years into retirement and has carried on with the support of The Luther Poets and appearances at The Adelaide Pub in Teddington.

My Poems
The war has shaken and stirred us all. We are all watching, hence 'Audience', and 'Kramatorsk station' was written after a specific incident. My poem, 'It goes on', I wrote towards the end of April because that's how it is. Who knows when it may end?

ANN VAUGHAN-WILLIAMS
Ann was born in Uganda. She lived there and attended school in Kenya until she was fourteen when her family returned to farming in Norfolk. Many of Ann's poems reflect the richness of her early experience. Ann has worked as a psychiatric social worker. She has taught Creative Writing and was a founder member of a writing group that meets weekly in Raynes Park library. Ann has two children and three grandchildren.

My Poem
My response to the Ukraine crisis comes from watching television and reading the newspaper. I have recently re-read 'A Short History of Tractors in Ukraine' by Marina Lewycka. This is a very entertaining book, which enlarges my perception of the country and its history.

CAROL **WAIN**
Carol is a retired social science lecturer who worked at Birkbeck, University of London. She has written poetry for much of her adult life. Several of her poems were published in 'Compassion,' a bereavement journal. This helped her to come to terms with the loss of her adult daughter who died in a car accident in 2000. Other of her poems appeared in 'Where The River Rests,' published in 2018 by Poetry Performance. Carol's father, a wartime RAF pilot, also wrote poems that were later published. She describes herself as a 'cat' person, who enjoys travel, art, history, music and photography. Since the outbreak of hostilities by Russia towards Ukraine Carol has been busy supporting various voluntary groups who are raising money to support Ukrainian refugees, including the Disaster Emergency Committee's national Appeal and Twickenham Town Hall.

My Poems
My poems reflect my understanding of personal and family loss. I've been moved by the many reports of this war since its outset, as shown on BBC Television News, plus Facebook and Instagram coverage.

'Ukraine—A Mother's Tale' and 'Finding A Way Out' are poems inspired by BBC News reports of the first 4-5 weeks of War in Ukraine. 'A Plea for Peace'—the need for peace in Ukraine is so apparent, crushing and yet a truce is still not begun, after months of war.

KEITH **WAIT**
Keith Wait has been known for some decades as a writer and as a drama and opera critic. He is currently editor of Mark Aspen Reviews and has been very active on the stage as actor, director and playwright. For many years this ran parallel with an earlier career in industry. Keith worked a quarter-century in oil and gas, as a chemist, chartered gas engineer and management consultant, most of this time being in international settings. He spent twelve years using his linguistic knowledge in compiling a technical dictionary in these fields, working mainly in Eastern Europe.

My Poem
The Iron Curtain represented a great divide in Europe, and I spent much time in the 1980's east of this line in compiling a dictionary of the gas industry, working with countries then under the hegemony of the USSR. Previously, I had consulted with the government of Greece in negotiating with Russia to buy gas from Gazprom, a name now familiar to all. I learnt the dynamics of the thinking of people in that part of the world.

My grandson Theo studied Russian in university and spent a lot of time in Russia and its satellites, working in the world of chess. He was stranded in Russia during the pandemic. We have come to know well Maria Emelianova, who is one of the brave Russian dissidents exiled from their homeland for speaking out against the regime and supporting the people of Ukraine. My poem is inspired by the courage of the Ukrainians and of their supporters who have lost so much.

IAN **LEE-DOLPHIN**

Ian Lee-Dolphin is a songwriter, poet, singer, guitarist and founder member of the bands Take Five, Zenith and French Lessons. Ian has been writing songs and poems since 1968 and played one of his first gigs at the Marquee in Wardour Street, London in 1970.

His two songs in this Anthology were inspired by the insane posturing of Vladimir Putin and his crazy decision to invade Ukraine.

Vladimir Putin is just one year older than me and we were both born in October and therefore we are both Librans. Librans are described as friendly people, concerned with attaining balance, harmony, peace, and justice in the world but regrettably Putin is an exception to this. While I am retired and enjoying life with family and friends, sad Vladimir feels the need to destroy towns and cities and kill thousands of people. He is following in a long line of power crazed rulers: Nero, Caligula, Vlad the Impaler, Genghis Khan, Attila the Hun, Ivan the Terrible, Hitler, Stalin and Pol Pot to name but a few.

MARGARET **MAY**

After taking a degree in Modern Languages and bringing up her family, Margaret spent most of her career in institutional publishing as an academic editor. She gained the CIOL Diploma in Translation and more recently a research degree in modern German literature. She especially enjoys translating modern German poetry; some of her work has been published online. Much of her own poetry was produced some years ago when she attended a women's creative writing group, but sharing her translations at Poetry Performance has coincided with a renewed interest in poetry about the humour of everyday life and ageing, and how it helps us keep a sense of perspective.

My Translated Poems
I was interested to know how German poets were responding to the Ukraine conflict and found Albert Ostermaier's powerfully urgent poem published online in the *Süddeutsche Zeitung;* it is movingly dedicated to a prominent Ukrainian fellow-writer, a long-standing friend of the author. Although Reiner Kunze's equally powerful poems relate to the conflict in Ukraine in 2014, they are just as relevant to the current situation, and 'Ukrainian Night' also resonates with historical allusions, particularly to the famous poem 'Todesfuge' [Death Fugue] by Paul Celan (who, like Rose Ausländer, was born in what is today part of Ukraine). Translating these three poems was both challenging and rewarding, and I have benefited greatly from insightful suggestions by various colleagues.

NOTES ON THE POEMS

Reiner Kunze
Diebeslied
Page 54
The epigraph is a quotation put together from several passages in Karl Schlögel's book 'Entscheidung in Kiew' [Decision in Kyiv], Munich, 2015 (pp. 40 and 74). (The English edition was published by Reaktion Books in 2018 as 'Ukraine: A Nation on the Borderland', translated by Gerrit Jackson.) This poem and 'Ukrainische Nacht' (p. 52) translated by Margaret May.

Chris Naylor
Chlorine and Aleppo
Page 61
The Russian General Alexandr Dvornikov, 'The Butcher of Syria' who was responsible for the destruction of Aleppo, has now moved to Mariupol.

Albert Ostermaier
Nach Kiew
Page 64
Albert Ostermaier's poem is dedicated to the Ukrainian writer and translator Yuriy Andrukhovych.
Translated by Margaret May.
https:// www.sueddeutsche.de/kultur/albert-ostermaier-nach-kiev-gedicht-krieg-ukraine-1.5541203, 4 March 2022

Fran Thurling
Kramatorsk station, Friday 8th April 2022
Page 68
At this time and place a Russian missile landed on Ukrainian refugees trying to leave by train.

Ian-Lee Dolphin
Get Out of Ukraine, President Putin
Page 77
Vlad, Bad and Dangerous to Know
Page 79
Both songs can be found on YouTube at:
https://bit.ly/3lLY12B